The Changing Face of CROMPTON

Frances Stott

Arts & Heritage Publications

OLDHAM
Education & Leisure

Acknowledgements

The author would like to thank the following people for the use of their photographs and for their information, advice and support:

Mr G.Abbott, Mrs E.Ballard, Mr A.P.Bennett, Bovington Tank Museum, Mr W.Brooks, Mr & Mrs G.Buckley, the late Mr H.Buckley, Mr E.Butterworth, Mr W.Cavanagh, Mr J.Chadwick, the late Mr J.Fountain, Mr & Mrs J.Gartside, Mr P. Gibson, the late Mr W.Goodwin, Greater Manchester Fire Service Museum, Mr P.Hirst & the Oldham Evening Chronicle, Mr B.Holland, Mr S.Langfield & Crompton Civic Trust, Mr & Mrs R.Lees, Mr J.Lowick, Mr R.Magee, Rev.A.Mashiter, Midland Bank, Mr & Mrs F. Miller, National Motor Museum at Beaulieu, Mr R.Prophet, Mr D.Potts, Road Locomotive Society, Royal Bank of Scotland, Mr J. Sikora, Mr M.Smith, Mr W.J.Smith, STORM, Mr.S.Sykes, Mr A.Travis, Mr K.Turner, Mr H.Ward, Rev. A.Wilson, Mrs M.Whyatt, the staff at Crompton Library and Oldham Museum and Mrs T. Berry and the staff at Oldham Local Studies Library.

Attempts have been made to trace the owners of all photographs used and the author wishes to apologise for any omissions which may have occurred.

Frances Stott is the Senior Community Librarian for the North of Oldham, which includes Crompton.

Published by Oldham Arts and Heritage Publications,
Local Studies Library, 84 Union Street, Oldham OL1 1DN
Tel: 0161 911 4654
ISBN 0-902809-38-5

Printed by Browns Colour Printers,
Units 4 & 5 Pennant Street, Oldham OL1 3NP Tel:0161 620 5547

Crompton, a small industrial town, once a centre of the cotton industry, with Shaw as its main village, lies at the very edge of Lancashire. The Pennine hills and Yorkshire are situated to the east, and Oldham three miles to the south. The name Crompton is derived from the Anglo-Saxon words "crom" or "crumb" meaning bowed or crooked, and "ton" a homestead or village. Shaw is also Anglo-Saxon in origin coming from the word "sceaga" meaning wood.

After the Norman conquest in 1066, Crompton was given to Roger de Pictaventis [or de Puicton]. A century later, the area, along with Belemore [Beal Moor] formed part of the district known as Kaskenemoor. It was held by Swain Fitz Alric and then his son Adam Fitz Swain. Roger de Montbegon and William Nevill married Adam's daughters and in 1212 held the estate equally, renting the property to various tenants. Gilbert de Notton later acquired the estate and in the

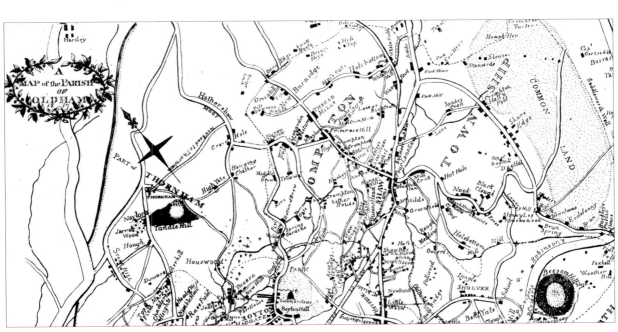

Coat of arms of the Crompton Family

early thirteenth century granted an area of Crompton [the first recorded use of the name] to the Abbey at Cockersand. In 1245 his grandson made a grant of land at Whitfield to the Hospitallers of St John of Jerusalem. The "Fee" of Crompton at this time was held by the De La Legh family, and it was Hugh De La Legh who changed the family name to Crompton.

Crompton was never granted manorial status but was made up of a collection of estates, owned by absentee landlords. It consisted of large areas of forest, moorland and swamp, upon which were a collection of small hamlets and farms. One hamlet, Shaw, was later to become the most important.

The number of inhabitants in the early fourteenth century has been estimated at no more than a dozen families, with the main tenants being the Traffords, Chethams, Chaddertons, Tetlows and also the Cromptons who by 1442 were occupying Crompton Hall.

Crompton from Butterworth's map of 1817

Holebottom Mill about 1880

The earliest evidence of the manufacture of textiles in the town is in 1474 when James Chetham leased Crompton Park to Edmund Brerelegh and part of the rent was "four dozen of cloth" to be woven by Brerelegh. A "dozen" was a piece of cloth $1 \frac{3}{4}$ yards wide by 12 or 13 yards long, which would have taken 15 workers one week to weave. The cloth would have been wool, probably from the local sheep which grazed on the moors. The manufacture of woollen cloth was still a cottage industry at this time, with the men weaving and the women spinning. By the late sixteenth century however, two mills were recorded in the town, at Holebottom and Millcroft. They probably employed no more than a dozen people.

Events in England during the sixteenth and seventeenth centuries impinged on life in Crompton. In 1569 as a result of a rebellion by the Earls of Northumberland and Westmorland, who tried to release Mary Queen of Scots from confinement at Tutbury, a muster roll of 73 citizens between the ages of 16 and 60 was compiled. These men could be called upon in times of war.

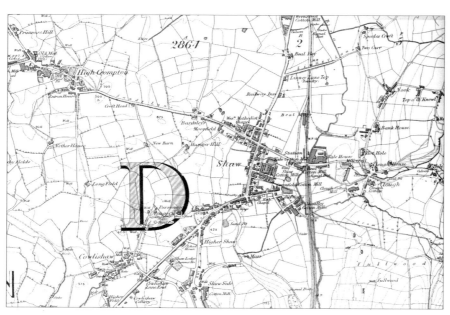

Crompton in 1840

Nineteen years later, at the time of the Spanish Armada, Thomas Crompton provided five armed men. Crompton did not escape the effects of the Civil War either; whilst most of the population appeared to support the King, Captain James Buckley of Whitfield Hall and his men were involved in the defence of Bolton when it was attacked by Royalists in 1643.

At the beginning of the seventeenth century Crompton was in the possession of thirteen landowners, five of whom probably lived in the town. In 1623 under the Enclosure Act, the common land was divided between them in proportion to the lands already held. Although there are no population figures for this time, a list was made in 1641 of those over the age of sixteen who were eligible to pay tax. From this it is possible to estimate the population as approximately 435. By 1714 the population had risen to 872.

The textile industry continued to grow and by the early eighteenth century there were woollen, linen, fustian and cotton weavers in the town. Between 1742 and 1762 six woollen manufacturers were recorded: Cocker at Birch Shaw; Smith at Shawside; James Wild at Beal Hey; James Milne at Rush Croft; Charles Howard also at Rush Croft and James Kershaw at Crompton Fold. During this period new homes were being erected, some three storeys high, the top storey being used as a loom room containing a spinning wheel, a spinning jenny and a loom.

Gradually the manufacture of cotton in Crompton became more important than wool, and by 1792 the woollen industry had died out. The invention of Kay's flying shuttle in 1733, Hargreaves' spinning jenny in 1767, Arkwright's water frame in 1769 and Crompton's spinning mule in 1779, together with the development of steam power allowed more cotton to be spun. This new machinery required more space and the factory system began to evolve. The earliest cotton mills were Travis and Milne at Low Crompton and Milne and Newton at Greenfield, Shaw.

Crompton from Higher Park about 1910.

In 1789 there was ten small factories spinning yarn which was still woven by cottage handloom weavers. The population continued to grow as people moved from the surrounding area to work in this expanding industry. By 1801 the population had grown to 3,482, and within the next thirty years it was to double. As the town expanded most of the new development took place in the "Newtown" area of Shaw.

By 1828 the number of factories had increased to 17 and included Milne and Travis at Shaw Lane; James Clegg's at High Crompton; Edmund Milne's at Mosshey and James Nield's at Littlewood. Coal mines which had existed as far back as the sixteenth century in Crompton, now expanded in number to 5 pits in order to satisfy the growing demand of the steam engines which provided the power in the mills.

These new factories however, along with the introduction of power looms, threatened the living of the hand loom weavers. They rioted in 1826 smashing 24 power looms in Clegg's mill at High Crompton. They continued with similar intent to Milne and Travis' mill at Newtown, but were unable to gain entry.

CROMPTON.

Mill		
Shaw Edge Mill ....Daniel Nield	1	12
Shaw Side ....J. Cocker	1	24
Cowlishaw ....Wilds	1	16
Cocker ....C. Barnett	1	6
High Crompton ......Cleggs, &c	1	25
Do. Do ....E. Whitehead	1	20
Do Do .....Clegg	1	20
Wood ....Milne	1	20
Crompton Fold ......Samuel Lord	1	14
Lane Side ....Brierley and Hamer......	1	7
Beile Bridge ....W. Taylor	1	20
Do Do ....Robinson and Co	1	20
Shaw ....Milne, Travis, & Milne...	2	60
Green Field ....E. Milne	1	24
Moss Hey ....Wilds	1	24
Clough ....J. Cheetham	1	21
	17	333
IN COLLIERIES.		
New Burnedge ......Buxton, Mills, & Co......	1	24
Total in the Township.	18	357

Left: A Table of the Steam Engines in Crompton and used in Cotton Mills and collieries in 1832.
Bottom: The old Greenfield Mill in 1905

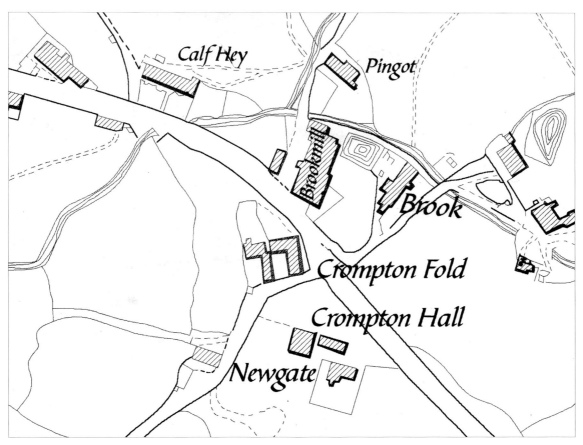

The area around Crompton Hall based on the Tithe Map of 1849

The expansion of the textile industry was also encouraged by improved communications. In 1805 work began on a new turnpike road. Intended to run from Hollinwood to Featherstall near Littleborough, it ultimately only stretched from Werneth to just beyond Jubilee. Jones Road [Buckstones Road] was constructed several years later to link it with the Oldham to Huddersfield Road. In 1863 an extension to the Oldham - Rochdale railway line was completed and Shaw station opened in December of that year.

The old road from Whitfield.

In the early 1860s, the cotton industry suffered a severe depression. The American Civil War had effectively stopped the supply of American cotton on which the mills were dependent. In 1863 there were only two mills working full time, three worked during the day and seven worked during the day with half the operatives. Eight were closed. To create more employment Crompton Local Board was formed in 1864 to raise loans to carry out public works.

After the American Civil War ended, trade improved. The Limited Liability Movement took a hold in 1874 resulting in the construction of Shaw Spinning Co. Ltd. Eleven other mills followed, and terraced houses were built to house the ever increasing number of workers and their families. Further expansion took place between 1901 and 1911 and the population of the town increased to a staggering 14,750 with reputedly "more millionaires to the square mile than any other place on earth".

Following the First World War there was a great demand for cotton goods but this was not sustained and by 1921 the industry again suffered a severe depression and many of the mills closed. From a peak of 36 mills in 1920 the industry declined until eventually the last cotton to be spun in Crompton was in 1989 at Lilac Mill, which closed in June 1989 and Park Mill, which closed in December of the same year.

Trent Mill under construction in 1907.

The demolition of Cape Mill in 1993.

Many improvements to the town have been proposed over the years including the redevelopment of the town centre in 1948. The proposal included a new swimming pool, Civic Hall, health and youth centres, a cinema complex and a by-pass, but the plans came to nothing. A new by-pass, Crompton Way, was constructed in 1969-1970 to reduce traffic passing through the town, which had increased as a result of the new M62 motorway two miles away.

Many of the disused mills have now been demolished and replaced by small industrial units and housing estates. Seven mills still remain, five of which are used as warehouses for mail order companies, providing employment for some of the 21,093 [1991 census] inhabitants of Crompton.

In 1974 Crompton became part of Oldham Metropolitan Borough and administrative control passed from Crompton Urban District Council to the new Borough Council. Some degree of local autonomy was returned in 1987 when Crompton was granted Parish Council status.

The Milne family Coat of Arms as displayed over the kitchen fireplace at Crompton Hall.

Shaw Chapel.

The origins of Shaw chapel are unclear but the first chapel was thought to have been called "St Patrick's on the Moor" and built of wood. The first record of its existence is from 1534 when Lawrence Hall was the priest. The chapel was rebuilt and enlarged in 1739 and again in 1797.

This third chapel [above] was opened in June 1800 and was described by the Rev. G. Allen in "Shaw Church in By-Gone Days" as being " a very plain, rectangular edifice built of rock-faced gritstone, with window dressings and keystones of ashlar" and "the western apex of the roof being surmounted by a hexagonal bell turret, crested with a wind vane".

In 1740 Shaw Society of Singers was formed to provide the chapel music, and a gallery with seats was erected for them at the west end of the chapel. Their reputation spread far and wide and during the late eighteenth century they travelled extensively giving concerts. Miss Deborah Travis, one of the Society's most notable members, became one of the most famous vocalists in the country. The Society finally wound up in 1883.

In 1835 Crompton became a separate parish, no longer tied to Oldham and Prestwich. The parish was divided in 1844 to form East Crompton Parish and again in 1878 to form High Crompton Parish.

Holy Trinity Church in the snow about 1895.

The Vicarage

A new church, "Holy Trinity", was built in 1870 to replace the old chapel, the site of which was marked by the shaft of an ancient cross. The foundation stone was laid by Mrs Mary Cocker of Shaw Edge on 24th May 1869 and the church was consecrated on Trinity Monday, 5th June 1871 by the Bishop of Manchester. It was built in the Gothic Decorated style, at a cost of £9,000. The burial tablets from the old chapel were preserved and placed in the new church.

Holy Trinity Church Vicarage was built in 1828 and used until 1956, when the present vicarage was constructed on Church Road. Prior to 1828 the vicars had occupied a variety of premises. The Rev. James Mashiter [1766-1795] had built Ivy Cottage on Oldham Road. His successor, the Rev. James Hordern Snr [1795-1819] did not live in the parish but resided at Failsworth Lodge and later Royton Hall, whilst the Rev. James Hordern [1823-1840] lived at Cowlishaw until the vicarage was built.

Shaw Church Anniversary Service on 9th July 1916
The church choir had been strengthened by the presence of these 120 or so singers, all dressed in white.

"The Queen Ann", Cheetham Hill in the 1890s. The building to the right belonged to John Hall who manufactured baskets and skips. According to the datestone on the pub, the Queen Ann had been in existence since 1760, but it is thought there may have been a pub in the vicinity prior to that. In September 1827 it was used for the first Petty Sessions in Shaw. The court was held in the concert room and the stables were used as the gaol. However the two prisoners held there absconded before the constables arrived to take them to Manchester.

The pub was rebuilt in 1924 and the entrance moved to Church Road.

Crompton Town Hall was opened on 28th December 1894 by John Wolstencroft, Chairman of Crompton Local Board.

Designed by Harold Cheetham in a Renaissance style, it was built in Ruabon brick with polished stone dressing and cost in the region of £4,000.

The Local Board had been formed in 1864 in order to combat the effects of the depression caused by the American Civil War. Local authorities were able to borrow money in order to carry out public works, so employing large numbers of out-of-work cotton operatives.

The first meeting of the Local Board was held on March 10th 1864 in the Blue Bell Inn, but future gatherings were held in the old school on High Street, which became the official Board offices.

As well as building the Town Hall, the Local Board was responsible for providing the town with a cemetery in 1891. When the Board became an Urban District Council in 1895 they constructed the Public Baths [1899] and Library [1906].

Crompton Library [below] was opened on 2nd February 1907 by J.W. Cockcroft, ex-chairman of Crompton Urban District Council. Prior to the opening, 150 people gathered at the Town Hall and processed via High Street and Market Street to Beal Lane. The front door of the Library was opened with a gold key presented to Mr Cockcroft by Mr James Horsfall, the architect.

The Library was built on land purchased by public subscription from Mr Abraham Clegg of Entron House and the building was constructed with £3,500 from the Carnegie Trust. The Library's initial collection of books came from Crompton Co-operative and Provident Society who donated their own library of 3,000 books.

The Carnegie Library was not the first library in the town. There had been a circulating library at Micklethwaite's printing establishment at 21 Market Street.

When it became obvious that the local burial grounds of Holy Trinity and St James' Churches were almost full, Crompton Local Board purchased 14 $\frac{1}{2}$ acres of land as a site for the cemetery from Messrs J.A. & J. Crompton. The cemetery was opened on 23rd October 1891 by John Wolstencroft, chairman of Crompton Local Board. The church portion was consecrated by the Bishop of Manchester on the same day. Three mortuary chapels were built: for the Non Conformists, the Roman Catholics and the Church of England. The former were demolished in the mid 1950s and the Church of England chapel was converted into a Chapel of Rest for all denominations.

Crompton Cemetery about 1910.

The "Big Lamp" at the turn of the century, with the King's Arms pub in the background.

Gas was first introduced into Crompton by the Oldham Gas Light and Water Works Company in 1830 when a small production plant was established off Greenfield Lane. Travis and Milne's factory in Newtown and a few shops were the first to be lit by gas on 18th September 1830. The Gas works were finally taken over by Oldham Corporation in 1853.

When gas street lighting was installed this extra-tall lamp was erected at the junction of the Oldham and Manchester Roads. It was pulled down on 17th June 1925 when electric lighting was introduced. Gas was still used to provide the majority of Crompton's street lighting until the mid 1950s.

High Street from the Big Lamp, looking towards the Hare and Hounds and White Lion public houses at the turn of the century. The village stocks, dated 1686, once stood opposite the White Lion and were moved to the cemetery and later Dunwood Park.

This area of Shaw, known as Sage Croft, was made up of numerous hovels which extended onto Shaw Lane [now High Street]. These hovels consisted of barns, stables and a smithy, complete with manure heaps, from which the drainage ran into an open stream alongside the road.

Much of the property seen here was demolished when Crompton Way was built in 1969-70.

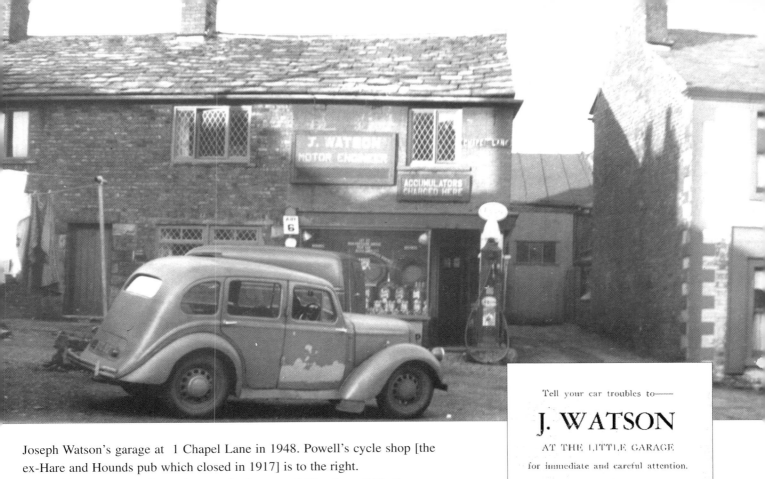

Joseph Watson's garage at 1 Chapel Lane in 1948. Powell's cycle shop [the ex-Hare and Hounds pub which closed in 1917] is to the right.

An old ash tree stood near here at the bottom of Cheetham Hill. It was a source of pride to the local inhabitants who used to decorate it with coloured flags and streamers at holiday time. It blew down on the 9th November 1887, and the wood was used by Mr Mellor, a clogger on High Street, to make a pair of clog soles which were exhibited in his shop window for many years.

Crompton's first school on Shaw Lane, now High Street. The building was used as offices by Crompton Local Board prior to the construction of the Town Hall. In 1897 it was sold by the Charity Commissioners for £200 and the money raised was invested. The resulting income was used to found a scholarship at Hulme Grammar School.

Although there were numerous private cottage schools in the area, the first public day school in Crompton [right] was not opened until 1791 when a plot of land was bought from John Milne of High Crompton. Subscriptions to pay for the actual building were raised in two days.

The school was originally only one storey high and the second floor was added in 1823. In 1838 a plot of land was bought on Manchester Road,

and a new school, Shaw National School was built. Several church schools then followed including Shaw Methodist School which was opened in 1842, St Mary's, High Crompton 1847 and St James' 1851.

The present site of the War Memorial on High Street in about 1910.

This land was purchased in 1913 with a view to Lancashire County Council building a technical school on the site. The scheme was eventually abandoned and the land bought by the War Memorial Committee. After the Memorial was constructed, the area facing High Street was landscaped, but it was not until 1924 that the Council drew up plans to landscape the rear section, which was used as allotments. The landscaping was carried out in 1925, and the garden opened on 14th June 1926 by Councillor S. Taylor, JP.

The War Memorial consists of a Scottish granite plinth surmounted by a large bronze statue flanked by two Rolls of Honour containing the 346 names of those from Crompton who died in the First World War. The statue represents "Man in the fullness of his strength, striding forward, helping on their way the future generation in the form of little children. He strikes through the teeth of brutal strife that threatens to rob them of the joy and beauty of existence, and, looking steadfastly to the future, he has striven to clear this peril from the way of life."

The monument, sculptured by Mr R.R. Goulden, was unveiled by Gen. Sir Ian Hamilton on Sunday 29th April 1923. Panels containing the names of those who died in the Second World War were added and unveiled by Councillor H.M. Turner on 12th November 1950.

A plaque commemorating those who served in the 1899 - 1902 South African wars is also in the Memorial gardens. Transferred in 1930 from the front of the Town Hall, it was unveiled on 25th June 1904 by Sir James Travis-Clegg, chairman of the War Fund Committee.

"Gun Week", 18th - 23rd November 1918 turned into "Thanksgiving Week", with the cessation of hostilities on November 11th. The Crompton Gun Committee aimed to raise £478,500 to invest with the Government and the week was to be the culmination of their efforts. On the evening of 18th November a six inch howitzer gun was brought from Shaw railway station, and a procession was formed, composed of scouts and other brigades and headed by Shaw Prize Band.

Throughout the week people monitored the savings effort on a barometer on the Town Hall [below]. The total amount raised was £607,100. Other donations by leading citizens brought the figure to £656,321, an average of £43 per head of population which earned Crompton the title of "Champions of the British Isles."

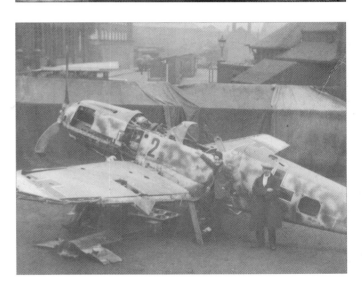

In May the following year, Crompton received a Mark IV tank in recognition of their war savings effort. After its arrival at Shaw station, it was driven to Dunwood Park where it remained until the Second World War, when it was used for scrap metal.

During the Second World War Crompton was again asked to contribute funds to the war effort. A Messerschmitt 109 fighter plane [above] was displayed on Crompton's Market ground for four days during October 1940. The aeroplane, shot down thirteen days previously, was exhibited in order to try to raise the £5,000 needed to purchase a Spitfire. At the end of the four days £118.13s had been collected, bringing Cromptons' Spitfire Fund to £1190 16s.

There has been a chapel on Refuge Street since 1835. In 1845 the United Methodists built a school and chapel here [above] which was used in 1859 by the Congregationalists and in 1874 by the Primitive Methodists.

By the turn of the century a new building was required. The old chapel was demolished and a new one constructed on the original site [below]. It was opened in 1902. When repairs became too expensive, in 1957, the Methodists moved out. Used as a warehouse for several years, the building was eventually demolished in 1967.

Four Lane Ends around 1890. The original Pineapple Inn can be seen in the background. The cottage in the centre has a shop to either side. No. 2, to the right was occupied by William Raine, the butcher, whilst No. 6 was occupied by Thomas Milnes, and it is his distinctive sign that can be seen above the doorway. The properties were demolished and replaced by new shops a few years later.

The Coach and Horses about 1888. The barn and brewhouse can be seen to the left of the pub on Beal Lane, whilst the shop to the right, No. 3, was used by a saddle maker. The Coach and Horses has been in existence from the late eighteenth century. It was from here in 1809 that Robert Mellor began the first coach service to Manchester. By the 1820s there were several coaches including the "Royal Defence", the "Industry" and the "Accommodation".

When this photograph [above] of the Coach and Horses was taken about 1892, William Hall
was the landlord and he had the pub refaced . As well as being a licensee, William had a funeral
and taxi service, and hired out wagons, dog carts, cabs [below] and private broughams.

·William Hall was also a pioneer in the use of new technology, whether it be hand-powered horse clippers or motorised transport .

William's car [above], thought to be a Belsize built in Clayton, Manchester about 1910. The original owners of the company were Marshall and Co., a cycle manufacturer, who built their first car in 1897. They changed their name to Belsize Motors Ltd. in 1901. The car was very popular for use as a taxi, which probably accounts for Hall's purchase. The Belsize company went bankrupt and closed in 1925.

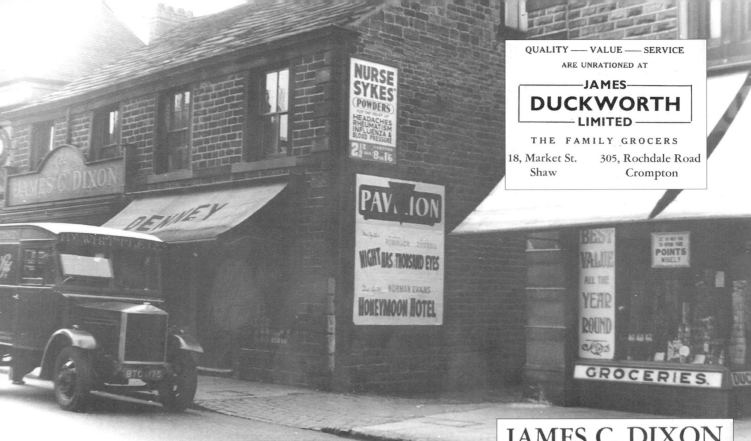

Market Street in 1948.

The shops from left to right are: Barclays Bank, James C.Dixon's, John Denny's, and James Duckworth's grocers shops. Duckworth's was built in 1893 on the site of Mary Pearson's tobacconist shop, behind which was Bingo Well, one of the chief sources of pure water before the days of reservoirs.

A quiet morning on Market Street about 1890.

The shop on the left is Butterworth's furniture shop [No. 38] next to it Butterworth's wringers and mangles [No. 36], and J.R. Collinge's butcher's shop [No. 34]. The double-fronted shop next door was occupied by James Hilton, fruiterer and greengrocer, who was also a herbalist and cow doctor. The next row of shops consisted of James Nall's hardware and ironmongers, followed by a tripe dealer, John Thomas Green, who also had the barber's shop next door. At the turn of the century these shops were pulled down and replaced by a new post office building, which is now occupied by a building society, a baker's, and a bank.

The Princes Cinema, Newtown Street.

The family of the late George Stott, plumber and painter, occupied these premises at the corner of Market Street and Milne Street in 1910. At one time they had been occupied by John Farrar, who as well as running an earthenware business, was the local postmaster.

The PICTUREDROME

ODDFELLOWS' HALL, SHAW

(FARROW STREET).

Proprietor - - T. W. HALL.

Always a Clean, Elevating, Instructive, and Up-to-date Programme;

Changed Entirely every Monday & Thursday.

71 Weeks without a break and a Reputation second to none.

The Hall has been newly beautified throughout, and we are installing an Electric Lighting Plant, when we shall be able to project Pictures equal —— to anything in the Country. ——

Afternoon Performances—TUESDAY and SATURDAY at 2-30.
Performance each evening at 8-15.
Saturday Evening—Two Performances, 7-0 and 9-0.

A WELCOME TO ALL.

Patrons not treated with civility, please acquaint the Management.

Crompton had three cinemas. The Pavilion was originally known as Shaw Picturedrome when it opened in 1911. The same owners ran the Electric Picturedrome which also opened in 1911 on the first floor of the Oddfellows Hall on Farrow Street. It was considered a fire risk and closed in about 1928. The Pavilion was to continue until the 1960s when it was converted into a bingo hall; it was demolished in 1994.

The Princes cinema opened in 1925 and continued to show films until its closure in 1958. It reopened three months later as a charity cinema, but ultimately closed in 1960. Converted into a theatre, it is now home to Crompton Stage Society.

Farrow Street in the early twentieth century. After consultation with the local inhabitants, Crompton Swimming Baths [left] were constructed and opened on 11th November 1899. Further up the street was Linley and Buckley, Engineers and Machinists later to become Oliver Machinery Co. The new Crompton library can now be found on this site.

To the right is Shaw Market. The origins of the market are unknown, but James Butterworth in his "Ancient History of Crompton" written in 1817, states that on Saturday's Market was displayed "some of the finest butcher's meat to be seen in any part of the county".

It has also been said that in the late nineteenth century, a market was held on the pavement in front of the Blue Bell Inn, which may account for the change of name from Shaw Lane to Market Street in the 1870s. By 1893 however the market was in its present location.

Market Street looking towards Four Lane Ends about 1910. The shop on the left is Arthur Schofield's newsagents [No. 16] which was started by his great uncle, Amos Ogden in 1840.

Two views of Market Street at the turn of the century. In 1901 the row of shops on the immediate right included Stott's plumbers, glaziers and decorators and James Stott's drapery business, next to the Duke of York public house.

On the opposite side of the road the shops included two drapers and a confectioners. The two rows of buildings were demolished in the 1970s and replaced by new shops with flats above.

T.Seymour Mead & Co. 76, Market Street. They provided groceries
and provisions in Shaw from the 1920s until the late 1960s.

67 Market Street has been in use as a chemist's shop
since 1799. It was originally owned by Robert
Thornton and later by Harriet Wall. In 1899 William
Yates took over the business. By 1968 it had expanded
into two of the new shops that were built on the site.

Beal Lane in 1901 soon after the clock tower was erected by the Co-operative Society on their premises, to celebrate their Golden Jubilee. The clock was made by Messrs W. Potts and Sons of Leeds and weighed 30 tons. The local authority paid for its illumination.

Crompton Co-operative and Provident Society Ltd. was formed in February 1851 when 12 men met in Joseph Sucksmith's home and agreed to open a provisions store. Their first shop was leased at Greenfield Gate and was stocked with various basic necessities such as flour, butter, lard, sugar and potatoes. Each of the founders took turns to serve in the shop which was at first only open three evenings a week. In 1852 a drapery department was added and in 1861 a clogger's shop.

The Co-op expanded to include numerous branches in the Crompton area including Marlfield in 1860, Heyside 1862, Beal Hey 1872, Higher Shaw 1874, Shore Edge 1875, Broadbent 1879, Rochdale Road 1896, Shore Lodge 1913 and Provident Park in 1920. Their new central premises on Beal Lane opened in 1867. It expanded again in 1909, with additional premises on Milnrow Road, which included a restaurant, bakery and jeweller's, and furniture and drapery shops in Park Street.

The Society was also involved in the construction of houses including Shore and Dingle Avenues and Park Parade on the Provident Park Estate in 1914.

The Co-op later moved to new premises at the corner of Four Lane Ends, and in 1967 their central premises were occupied by W. Foy's hardware shop. This building was destroyed in a dramatic fire in 1982.

Beal Lane at the turn of the century. On the left, Vale Mill owned by the Crompton Spinning Co. Ltd. who had taken over from James Taylor in 1874. It ceased production and was demolished in 1934. To the right is the site of Briar Mill, which was built in 1906.

Grains Road in the early 1960s, with Lily Mill chimney on the left and Rutland Mill chimney on the right. These properties, some of which were built as early as 1778, were demolished soon after this photograph was taken. The footpath to the right later became Hillside Avenue.

The cottage on the left was the birthplace of Philip Gilbert Hamerton [September 1834], He later became well-known as an author, artist and art critic. Philip's mother died two weeks after his birth and ten years later, on the death of his father, [a solicitor], he went to reside permanently with his aunts at Burnley, having already spent much of his early life there. After studying art in London, he went to France, returning to spend four years in the Scottish Highlands. Much of his later life was spent in France where he died on 3rd November 1894. His published works include "Etchings and Etchers" "Life of Turner" and "Imagination in Landscape Painting". In 1911 his widow presented a collection of his works to Crompton Library, where they are still housed.

Laneside around 1900

St. George's School [left] was designed to accommodate both Infant and Junior children and to provide space for a Sunday School. The foundation stone was laid on 26th September 1896 by Mrs Lees-Milne. The school was formally opened on 24th July 1897 by Miss Crompton, but it was not used as a Sunday School until January 1898, nor as a Day School until later that year.

The school was replaced in 1967 by a building on the opposite side of Scarr Lane, and opened on 23rd July by Mr and Mrs Frank Everington.

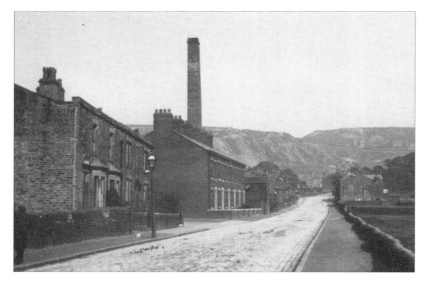

Buckstones Road was called Jones Road until the 1850s and was built as a toll road around 1810 to link the Oldham-Huddersfield Road at Grains with the new road from Werneth to Jubilee. There were three toll gates or bars. One was situated to the right of this photograph, at Calf Hey, whilst the others were above Doghill and at Grains Bar.

East Crompton St James' Mission Room was situated in the old loom lofts of the three-storey cottages in the centre of the photograph [below]. The Mission was eventually replaced by St Saviour's Church. The cottages were badly damaged and had to be demolished after the floods of 1964, when water from the Brook, and overflow from Brushes Clough Reservoir, cascaded down Buckstones Road.

Looking down Buckstones Road towards Crompton Fold. The entrance to Crompton Hall is on the left and the Brook Mill chimney can be seen in the background.

St Saviour's Church [above], built on the site of Brook Mill. The land had been given by Mr James Lees-Milne and the church was built with money given by Miss Mary Crompton of New Bank.

On the day of its dedication by the Bishop of Manchester [2nd November 1908], a procession of 1,500 people left East Crompton St James' School and proceeded along Milnrow Road, Goats, and Buckstones Road which were all decked with bunting.

High Crompton Brass Band headed the procession followed by the scholars and congregation with the school banner. The congregation from St George's and the worshippers of the Crompton Fold Mission followed. Below can be seen at the rear of the procession with the choir of St James, the Rev S. Williamson and other vicars of the town.

OPENING OF ST SAVIOURS

NO 5

Crompton Fold around 1930. The tower of Crompton Hall can be seen emerging through the trees. Shore Edge Chapel, top left, was built by the local Primitive Methodists in 1873 to replace their original 1839 "Ebenezer Chapel". St Saviour's Church can be seen bottom left, with Buckstones Road cutting through the centre of the photograph.

Crompton Hall

The first Crompton Hall was known to have been in existence in 1442 and was owned at that time by Thomas de Crompton and his family. It was thought to be a typical medieval building, with a central hall, open to the rafters and probably two-storey sections at each end. The Hall remained with the Crompton family until the death of Thomas Crompton in 1608, when the estate passed to his three daughters. In 1692 the Hall was occupied by Hugh and Alice Yannes and later by a John Kershaw and his wife.

The old Hall was demolished around 1848 when Alice Milne [née Crompton] bought the property, so reuniting the estate with the family. Alice, in 1814 had married James Milne of Park House who died in 1823. The rebuilt Hall, [previous page] incorporated some of the fifteenth century oak panelling from the previous Hall as well as a magnificent open fireplace, built around 1440.

In 1950, Mr Edward Leigh, then the owner of the hall, sold it to a demolition firm. A bungalow now stands on the site.

The Drawing Room at Crompton Hall.

The Hall under demolition in March 1952.

Shore Edge. The Co-operative Society's branch store, seen here, was opened in 1875.

"The Slater's Arms" around the turn of the century when Barlow Garside was the landlord. The pub has been in existence from the 1820s, before then it was probably a farmhouse. For a short period of time during the late 1830s it was called the "Boilermaker's Arms". It closed around 1952 and was later demolished.

Near to the "Slater's Arms" was a building known as the "Town's House", left to the Parish by one of the Percivals of Royton Hall and used as an annexe to the workhouse on Oldham Road.

Brun Chapel, Buckstones Road, was built in 1823 by the Wesleyans of Moorside. According to Ammon Wrigley "it was badly needed, for at that time and for years after it was closed, a Shore Edge and Doghill Sunday was the devils own day for drinking, gambling, cockfighting, wrestling and pigeon flying." It later became a Mission Room for Shaw Chapel before it was handed over to the new parish of East Crompton on the 6th July 1845. They held services here for two years until their own church was built, shortly after which the chapel closed, and the font was transferred to East Crompton church. The chapel was subsequently used as a barn and in 1996 it was converted into a house.

The inscription over the doorway reads:

Methodist Chapel
Erected A.D. 1823
O Lord we beseech the, send now profperity
Pfalm 118th Verfe 25th

Milnrow Road from Four Lane Ends at the turn of the century. The Pineapple Inn stands to the left, whilst the building lower down the road, with the steps leading to the upper storey, was used by the Methodists for their Sunday School. The buildings below were situated on the corner of Duck Street [now King Albert Street] and in 1910 were used as a joiner's shop by Joseph Street. An undertakers now stands on the site.

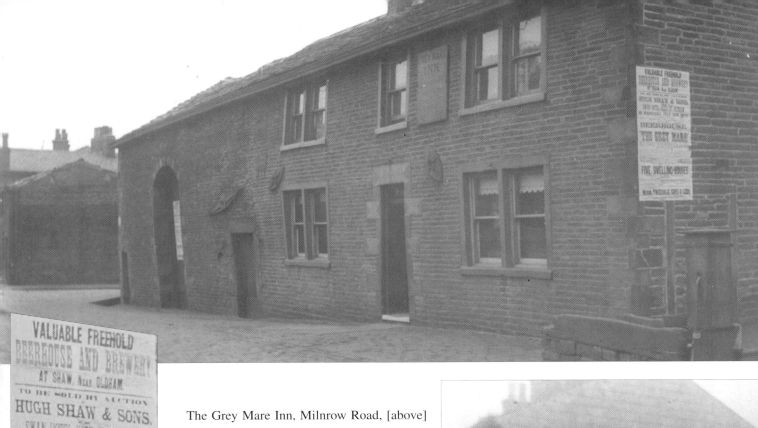

The Grey Mare Inn, Milnrow Road, [above] in 1902, when William Stott was the landlord. This building started life as a farmhouse and became a pub in about 1840. It obtained its water supply from the pump outside. The site has now been occupied by a garage for sixty years.

Right: The site of Shaw Brass and Electro Plating Co. at 20 Milnrow Road. Originally a two-storey building, it was later reduced to one-storey. The building was demolished in 1909 to allow for the expansion of the Co-op.

Milnrow Road, [below] around 1910, with an open top tram. Behind it, on the right, is the Grey Mare pub.

Taken about the same time [1910], but lower down Milnrow Road. St James' School can be seen to the left.

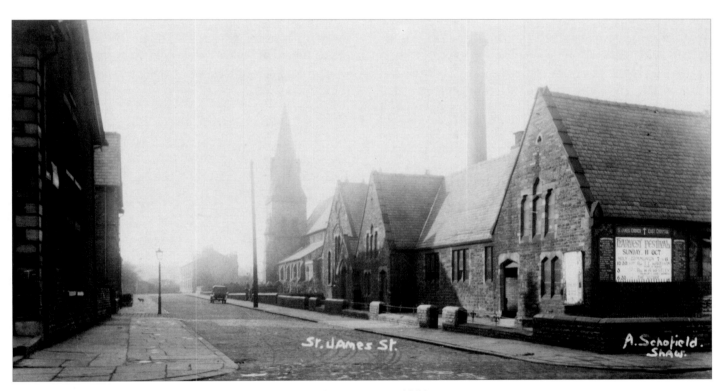

St James Street in 1914

East Crompton Parish was created on 13th December 1844 and as it had no church, services were held at Brun Chapel on Buckstones Road. The foundation stone of the church, which can be seen above, was laid on 25th July 1846 [St James' Day] by Mrs Milne, and it was consecrated on 6th July 1847 by the Bishop of Chester. The spire and tower were not added until about 1867.

St James' School, to the right, had been built in 1851 and an Infant department added later. Space became a problem, so it was decided to build a separate Infant School on the other side of the church in 1905. In 1938, with a view to building a new school, the chief rent for a site on Salt Street was purchased. However the new Primary School was not constructed until 1964. It was opened on 25th July of that year by Mr and Mrs Leslie Barker. The Church Institute, on the left, first met in the school, and then over a shop in Milnrow Road before finally moving into their own premises in 1883. The building was demolished during the construction of the by-pass in 1969.

Wren's Nest Mill around 1910. The mill was also called 'Barbers Mill' and was built approximately 50 years earlier by the Shaw Mill Company. In 1889 it was occupied by Jonathan Wild. The mill was destroyed by fire in 1920 and the site was purchased by Councillor Sir William Hopwood who presented it to Crompton Council for use as a public recreation ground. St Edmund's Roman Catholic Chapel of Ease and Parish Centre which opened in 1972, now stands on the site.

Hawk Mill, also about 1910. The post box is the same one as seen in the previous photograph. Sutcliffe's clothes stall is in the foreground. Hawk Mill was constructed in 1908 by the Hawk Mill Co. Ltd . It was taken over twice before ceasing production in 1967, after which it was used by a company making stretch covers. The top two storeys were removed in 1976 and the rest of the building was demolished in 1991. The site is now used for housing.

Smallbrook Road [above] about 1900, looking towards Wren's Nest. The Commercial Inn can be seen in the background along with Wren's Nest Mill chimney. Smallbrook Road formed part of the original road from Shaw to Rochdale via Whitfield, until the turnpike road via Jubilee was built in 1805.

On Sunday 20th September 1908 a heavy rainstorm occurred in the Crompton area. The River Beal overflowed, flooding the surrounding fields.

At Goats the water washed away the ballast of the Lancashire and Yorkshire railway line and covered the tracks. At Smallbrook [right] many of the houses were flooded and furniture washed out. At Smallbrook Mill, damage was caused to the yarn.

However Clough Mill suffered the most damage. Water from the nearby brook poured into the yard and cellar of the new mill where thousands of new cops were stored. Bales of cotton and cloth were also damaged and the weaving shed was the only part of the mill still able to operate.

Crompton Spinning Company's cellar and cardroom were flooded to a depth of eighteen inches while Mosshey Mill and the surrounding area was under two feet of water. Other mills were more fortunate with only a few inches of flooding. Shops in Market Street also had their cellars flooded.

Dunwood Park was presented to the Council by Captain Abram Crompton JP and his nephews on 22nd June 1911, Coronation Day. It opened to the public [below] on 14th September 1912. A plaque commemorating this event can still be found at the Bridge Street entrance to the park [above]. Comprising 20.66 acres, the southern end of the park and the area along the valley were laid out as a typical Edwardian park complete with bandstand, bowling green, children's play area and tennis courts. Trees were planted by Crompton Council in 1912 and Lancashire County Council in 1957.

Mr R. R. Goulden sculptured not only a War Memorial for Crompton but also this drinking fountain [below]. It was installed in Dun Wood Park in 1925 and bore the inscription "This fountain is placed here as a mark of appreciation of the self-sacrifice and devotion of the women of Crompton during the Great War. Help one another!" Unfortunately it was stolen in April 1968.

Crompton Urban District Council.

SHAW PRIZE BRASS BAND

DUN WOOD PARK,
SUNDAY, MAY 23, 1926.

AFTERNOON PROGRAMME, 3-0 to 5-0.

1. HYMN—Tune *Silver Hill* ....
2. MARCH .... "Simplicity" .... *Hume*
3. OVERTURE .... " King's Lieutenant " .... *Moore*
4. EUPHONIUM SOLO "Gipsy's Warning " .... *Hartmann*
           Soloist—Mr. JAMES KAY.
5. SELECTION ...." Maritana " .... *Wallace*
6. PRELUDE............. "Rachmaninoff " .... *Arr. by Rimmer*
7. SELECTION .... " Talisman " .... *Balfe*
8. LARGO .... " The Celebrated " .... *Handel*
9. HYMN ....

NATIONAL ANTHEM.

Conductor   -   -   Mr. W. EASTWOOD.

Harry Milne, Printer, Market Street, Shaw

Rushcroft in the 1930s.

At the top of the photograph can be seen Park [1834-1991] and Woodend Mills [1859-1968]. To the right are Wye Mill No. 1 built in 1914 and Wye Mill No. 2 which was the last mill to be constructed in Crompton in 1925. Both mills were demolished in 1974 after remaining empty for several years. Behind them is Smallbrook Mill [1875-1964]. These mill sites have been redeveloped for housing. To the left is Trent [1908-1967/9] and Duchess Mill [1884-1935]. Their sites are now occupied by an industrial estate. In the foreground is Crompton Cricket Club.

Park House [above] with Milnrow Road and the railway line below. The land on which Park House stands was originally owned by the Crompton's of Crompton Hall and later the Percival's and Radcliffe's of Royton Hall. They sold it to James Milne whose family had resided at nearby Top o' th' Hill [right] since at least 1553. The cottages had been used as loom-houses prior to the building of the mill at Park, at the end of the 19th century.

James' son married Alice Crompton in 1814, and after his death in 1823, she, along with her brothers Abel and Abram continued the cotton business as A. & A. Crompton & Co. Right: Top o' th' Hill now known as Higher Park.

Jubilee around 1910 with the River Beal to the left.

The road in the background was built by James Milne of Park House and William Clegg of Westwood, after the setting up of the Dryclough, Shaw and Rochdale Turnpike Trust in 1805. The original intention was to construct a road from Hollinwood to Featherstall near Littleborough with several branch roads leading from it. The road was never completed in its entirety, only sections of the road from Werneth to Royton and Shaw, and from Wren's Nest to Newhey were finished.

John Milne also constructed the cottages at Jubilee and the public house, which had originally been built on the other side of the road. It was moved when the railway was constructed in 1863.

The hamlet of Whitfield which lies nearby was built on the old road to Rochdale. It was approached by a steep hill from Shaw and there was always a chain-horse stationed at the foot of the slope to help heavily laden wagons. At one time Whitfield was the most important hamlet in Crompton with over 40 householders and several shops including a grocers, chemists, alehouse [left] and a smithy. John Hall's house was registered as a Dissenter's meeting place in 1703 and again in 1763. It was to this Quaker family that George Travis was apprenticed at the end of the eighteenth century. Sent to learn the craft of loom making, he later married Hall's daughter, Ann and went on to become a fustian manufacturer at Heyside. His descendants became successful cotton spinners in Crompton.

Whitfield Hall Farm around 1972.

Eighty acres of land at Whitfield once formed a grant of land made by Gilbert de Barton to the Hospitallers of St John of Jerusalem in 1243. Whitfield Hall is mentioned for the first time in the sixteenth century at which time it was occupied by the Buckley family, who lived there for 200 years. One of them, Captain James Buckley was involved in the defence of Bolton against the Royalists in 1643. In 1666 the Hall was the largest house in Crompton. The Hearth Tax records list it as having five hearths whilst Crompton Hall had only two. In the early eighteenth century it was sold to the Levers of Alkrington, who in turn sold it to their tenant, Mr Milne, in 1786. In 1907 the Rev. G.Allen reported that only a portion of the Hall remained, the porch and two wings had been dismantled and what was formerly the rear of the house rebuilt to form a new front elevation.

Rochdale Road about 1910 [above]. Taylor's grocers shop is on the left, whilst James H. Broadbelt's plumbers and decorators is to the right. The shops were demolished in the 1920s and the site used for the present-day Post Office, which until then had been situated at various sites on Market Street and Rochdale Road.

The first Post Office in Crompton was established in 1843 at William Wild's greengrocers shop in Sandy Lane [Rochdale Road], opposite the Pineapple Inn. After his death, his wife moved it to Market Street prior to it being taken over by John Farrar of 57 Market Street. It was transferred to his house at 13 Rochdale Road [above right] in the 1880s, where it was to remain for several years. By 1884 it was run by John Pollitt at 5 Market Street until the Post Office Buildings were erected at 30 Market Street. Finally in 1925 it moved back to Rochdale Road.

Joe Mellor's house on Durden Street. Joe was a coal dealer in the 1890s, and in the 1920s was registered as a carrier.

The site of the London City and Midland Bank [above left] on Rochdale Road. The bank, which amalgamated with the Oldham Joint Stock Bank Ltd. of Market Street, outgrew their original premises and purchased 14 and 16 Rochdale Road in 1895 in order to build a new branch. They moved into this new bank, [above], in 1897. The bank closed in late 1992 and the building is now used as a wine bar.

Thomas E. Raine's butchers shop [inset] at the corner of St Mary's Gate and Rochdale Road had originally been a cloggers shop owned by James Wild. In 1925 the site [above] was bought by William Deacon's Bank in order to build a new branch, which was completed in 1928.

There are records of the Wesleyan Methodist Movement in Shaw as far back as 1790. In 1811 they had established a Sunday School in a room above the Woolpack Inn on Market Street. The school later moved to the Newtown area and finally into a first floor room in a building at the bottom of Duck Street [now King Albert Street].

In 1815 the Methodists erected their own chapel [below] on Sandy Lane [now Rochdale Road]. Mr James Cheetham of Clough laid the foundation stone on the 22nd June. The chapel, named "Bethel" was opened the following year and was used jointly as a chapel and school. It had a semi-octagonal gallery from which it was said "every auditor therein has a full view, if not of the pulpit, at least of the preacher". The seats on the lower floor were formed on the same plan as the gallery. A separate school, at the rear of the building, was constructed in 1831 and rebuilt in 1872.

The chapel was enlarged in 1863. Designed by James Simpson of Leeds it has a classical facade. The Chapel is no longer used for religious purposes.

Bardsleys, at the corner of Glebe Street and Rochdale Road in about 1900. The building dated back to 1695.

Orchard House [above] was occupied in 1817 by Samuel Milne, who was renting part of Clegg's Mill in 1813. In 1930 the outbuildings to the left were demolished to make way for the straightening of Rochdale Road. The house itself was pulled down several years later, and in the mid 1960s bungalows were built on the site.

The house probably took its name from the field next door; "The Orchard". John Milne who lived by the Orchard at High Crompton ran a private school at the end of the eighteenth century. It was he who, in 1791, provided the land for the building of Shaw School.

"Bottom o' th' Fold" was next to Orchard House. The road seen running in a semicircle in front of the cottages shows the old course taken by Rochdale Road. After the new section of road was cut alongside Orchard House this old road was renamed "The Orchards". The house seen behind and to the right of the cottages is "Bank House", built in 1922 for the manager of William Deacon's Bank. The house is still there, whilst the cottages have been replaced by bungalows.

High Crompton in the late 1920s, with Thornham Lane running from left to right and, at its junction with Rochdale Road, the Post Office. The mills seen here are those owned by the Clegg family, whose company was founded at the end of the eighteenth century. In 1855 the firm was split in two, with Joseph Clegg & Co. being responsible for Springhill Mill [demolished 1938] on Thornham Road [centre], two new mills to the south, and Old Brox Mill which was situated on the vacant site top centre of the picture. Joseph Clegg's ceased production in 1975 and the mills were demolished the following year.

John Clegg and Sons meanwhile were responsible for New Mill, just off this photograph to the right. This was burnt down in 1929 and the site is now used for housing. The Clegg family built many of the fine mansions that once graced Rochdale Road: West Hall, Croft Head and Hill Crest [originally called Stoneleigh]. They were also the benefactors of St Mary's Church which is at the top of the photograph. The house with gardens on Rochdale Road is Primrose Hill, originally home to a branch of the Milne family, mill owners within the town. It was demolished in the early 1960s.

The Old Brox Mill or Old Mill [above] was built in the late eighteenth century by the Clegg family. It was rebuilt in 1819 after a disastrous fire. In 1826 it was attacked by power loom wreckers who destroyed 24 looms, and in 1842 by plug pullers. It was demolished about 1906.

The mill at one time had three chimneys. The last one [above right] was demolished on 20th October 1906 by the steeplejack William Brown. A large crowd gathered to watch him place paraffin-soaked timbers against the base of the chimney, which were then ignited by his grandson. The chimney was 120 feet high and had been built about 50 years previously.

High Crompton Post Office [above] around 1905. There has been a Post Office here since 1897. It is seen here surrounded by the terraced houses of mill operatives who worked at the nearby Clegg's mills.

The Post Office was decked out in coloured bunting to celebrate George V's Silver Jubilee in 1935. Crompton Town Hall, and the War Memorial were similarly decorated. Various events were held in the town to commemorate the Jubilee, including a children's procession, a religious service on the Market Place, tea for the over-70s and a spectacular bonfire and fireworks on Doghill in the evening.

Rochdale Road, High Crompton.

To the left, at the corner of Wood Street is the Co-op store. At the front of the shop was a butchery and grocery department, at the rear was a greengrocers and upstairs there was a cloggers and shoe repairers.

The large three-storey building in the centre was originally the loom house of William Fielding. He was declared bankrupt in 1793 and his goods, including three pairs of looms and a spinning jenny, were sold to pay off his debts. At the time this photograph was taken the building was being used as a shippon by the farm at the rear. To the left of the shippon are the walls and railings of Primrose Hill House, originally the home of John Milne and his family. He was a partner in the spinning company of Milne, Travis and Milne, and was reputed to have owned the first carriage in the town.

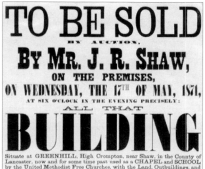

The first United Methodist Church at Greenhill was erected on Moss Gate Road in 1847, ten years after the foundation of the Sunday School. Twenty years later the church-school was already proving to be too small and a proposal was made to build a new church at the corner of Rochdale Road and Moss Gate.

The foundation stone of the new church was laid on 4th June 1870 by Mr J.M. Cheetham of Woodend, and opened on 10th May 1871. Attempts to sell the old chapel evidently failed and it was rented out, eventually to become a shippon for Greenhill Farm. In 1961 a building fund was launched for a new church and the following year a site was bought on the new Higher Rushcroft estate. The old church closed on 25th August 1963 and in the three year interim before the new church of St Andrew's opened [16th July 1966], services were held in St Mary's, High Crompton. The old church was sold for demolition and a bungalow was built on the site.

Oldham Road [above] about 1900, before the arrival of the trams. The house with a garden to the left is Ivy Cottage, which was built by the Rev. James Mashiter about 1770. Shawside Mills can be seen in the background, and, where the two gentlemen are standing, the Kings Arms.

The first Roman Catholic church in Crompton since the Reformation was established in 1874 in an old mill which had been used by fustian cutters. The first mass was celebrated by Father Charles Grymonprez who had led a procession from St Mary's in Oldham to Shawside.

A purpose-built church and school [right] was constructed on the foundations of the old mill in 1896 and opened in May by the Bishop of Salford. A club room and sacristy were added two years later, followed by an institute and church hall in 1921. A Chapel of Ease, St Edmund's, was opened at Wren's Nest in 1972 and a replacement church at Shawside was opened in March 1984 on the site of the church institute. When Our Lady's Secondary Modern School opened in Royton in 1961, St Joseph's was used as a Primary School only. A new school for infants was opened in 1972 followed by a Junior school in 1975.

Manchester Road [above] around 1910, looking towards Shaw, with Dawn Mill chimney in the background. The spire to the right belongs to Shaw National School built in 1839 to replace the old school on High Street. It was extended in 1896. The school closed in 1969 and the pupils transferred to the former Crompton Central School on Kings Road, which was then renamed Newbarn. The old school was demolished and town houses now stand in its place.

Shaw National School

The Royal Oak, Cowlishaw first appears in licensing records in 1808. The school on High Street was transferred here around 1823 whilst the school was being enlarged. George Varley, whose name appears above the door was licensee between 1900 and 1917.

Bank House Colliery on Grains Road [below] owned by the Oldham, Middleton and Rochdale Coal Company, closed in 1905. It had it's own spur line from the Oldham-Rochdale railway track.

Coal mining in Crompton is recorded as far back as the sixteenth century. Among those who paid rent in Crompton in 1522 was Richard Wylde "for getting cowles at Lennardyne [near Crompton Fold] 16 quarters......16d." The next coal pits recorded were at Low Crompton and Holebottom. The industry grew as demand increased from the expanding cotton industry.

At the beginning of the nineteenth century there were reputedly eleven pits, although only five, employing a total of thirty-two colliers, are mentioned in the Valuations of 1828. Ordnance Survey maps record pits at Park, Brook, Old Brook, Holebottom, Clough, Jubilee, Bank House, Low Crompton, Browns, Crow Knoll and Burnedge. Crompton Moor is honeycombed with old mine workings, some over 200 years old. There were many thin coal seams, some only inches thick, outcropping on the hillside, making it easier to tunnel horizontally rather than sink a shaft.

During the nineteenth century coal was delivered to a terminus behind the Union Bank on Market Street from a pit at Dingle, just past Fullwood. The horse-drawn coal wagons were brought by a tramway [or sill road]. Later the sill road terminated at a depot near the Moss Hey gas works.

Jubilee Colliery [right] was founded in 1845 by the Edge Lane and Dryclough Colliery Co. to obtain coal from the Mountain Mine seam 325 feet below ground. In the 1870s it was owned by the Oldham, Middleton and Rochdale Coal Co. who in the 1880s also owned Low Crompton Mine. In 1883 it was purchased by Platt Bros. and Co. Ltd. who used the coal to produce coke for the Company's iron works in Oldham. It had it's own railway siding. The mine closed in 1932.

Shaw Mill, Newtown, [left] built about 1820 by Milne, Travis and Milne. In 1830 the mill was lit by gas and by 1832 it was powered by two steam engines. It was taken over by John Clegg and Son who ran the mill until its closure in the 1890s.

In 1901, Dawn Mill, [below] designed by P.S. Stott was constructed on the site.

Lilac Mill [right] under construction in 1914. Lilac Mill collapsed whilst being built, in gale force winds on 14th September 1914. Fortunately the workforce of 200 had finished for the day. The whole building fell to the ground with such a crash that it was heard for miles around. Many of the pillars snapped and these, along with all the bricks, girders and beams ended up piled in a heap in the foundations.

Work had been due to start the following day on concreting the roof. All the pillars had been bolted and braced together and formed a framework weighing approximately 2000 tons. The brickwork had been started at both ends of the mill and a portion of the second and third storey. The mill was rebuilt and in March 1918 requisitioned for use as an aircraft factory, assembling components. It reverted to a cotton mill in 1919.

Ash Mill also fell during its construction, two months prior to completion in 1883.

The remains of Lilac Mill [right] on 15th September 1914. Briar Mill can be seen in the background.

Lyon Mill fire in 1911.

Lyon Mill suffered two serious fires. The first major fire broke out on 6th July 1911 and destroyed the top two spinning rooms. The four pairs of mules on each floor were completely destroyed. Two "steamers", [above] and two tenders from Oldham fire brigade attended the fire. All the fire engines from Oldham were eventually called out in order to save the mill from being completely destroyed.

The second fire occurred on 17th April 1929 and completely gutted the building. It was discovered at 12.15pm when most workers were at dinner. The fire had started on the second storey and was thought to have been caused by friction in machinery in the card room. Within one hour the whole mill was alight. Of the five-storey building, only the south and part of the west wall [right] remained standing. The winding and beaming section at the south-west corner, the offices and the engine house were saved. As a result of the fire, over 200 operatives lost their jobs.

The ruins of Lyon mill after the fire in 1929.

A standard four-wheeled double-decked tram car built by Dick, Kerr and Co., with extended canopies and reversed stairs. Single decked cars were also used on the routes.

The first sets for the electric tramway which ran from Higginshaw via Heyside to Shaw, Wren's Nest, were taken up near Shaw Edge on 27th July 1904 by the Chairman of the Council, Councillor J.W. Cockcroft JP. The route was constructed by Messrs Wm. Underwood of Dukinfield for Crompton Urban District Council who then leased the line to Oldham Corporation. After the new track had been inspected, the tram service commenced on 15th November 1904. Two days later the service was extended to Chadderton Road.

When a second line from the centre of Shaw via Manchester Road to Royton was opened on 13th April 1905, a through service to Werneth commenced. The service was extended to Wren's Nest [sharing the same terminus as the Chadderton Road - Shaw service] on 1st December 1919 and to

Hollinwood in January 1921.

When the route number boxes replaced the coloured light system in 1921, the Chadderton Road - Shaw service became the No. 9 route and the Hollinwood - Shaw service the No. 8. Plans to extend the lines to the railway station and High Crompton did not materialise.

The No. 9 tram route closed and was replaced by buses on 11th June 1935 and the No. 8 route closed on 2nd December 1939.

Middle: An open topped, double-decker tram car on Milnrow Road about 1908.

Bottom: Tram cars on Milnrow Road at the Wren's Nest terminus.

Shaw and Crompton station about 1960.

The railway line from Oldham to Rochdale via Shaw was opened to goods traffic in August 1863 and to the public on Monday 2nd November 1863. The track had taken three years to construct and cost £350,000. An extensive goods yard and cotton warehouse were also provided. Diesel trains first entered service on the the line in 1958 and in the 1980's "Pacer" and "Sprinter" trains were introduced. There were three spur lines from the main track; to Jubilee Colliery, Bank House Colliery and Park and Woodend Mills. The goods yard closed in 1963 and the station's buildings were demolished in 1973.

Left: The station with the cotton warehouse in the background.

William C. Taylor's Foden 1489 steam lorry, complete with an old horse trailer, outside John Ashworth's blacksmith's shop on Milnrow Road [opposite the Grey Mare pub]. The steam lorry had been bought by Taylors in 1907 but was scrapped in October 1924 when they purchased a replacement. Taylor's were a haulage contractor based at 2 Cheetham Street, Clough. By 1909 the blacksmith's shop had been taken over by Samuel Shelmerdine.

Stephen Gilks, Motor Haulage Contractor of Hope Street, with two of his Yorkshire steam wagons about 1914. The engine on the left was bought by Gilks in March 1912, whilst the engine on the right was purchased in 1913. The firm had three more Yorkshire steam wagons built in 1914, 1918 and 1919 respectively. In 1921 the firm became Butterworth and Gilks. Both of the steam wagons above were sold to the Failsworth Transport Company in 1929.

A Temperance Society outing about 1910. The Temperance Society had become active in the 1880s to preach that temperance not abstinence was the goal of the society. The Society held services in different parts of the town, sometimes in the open air, sometimes in factories. This outing was in a Thornycroft wagon loaned by Shaw Motor Carrying Company. They were accompanied by the Band of Hope, the women's section of the organisation.

Watching St Joseph's Church process at Four Lane Ends on Whit Friday. The stables of the Coach and Horses where Crompton's ambulance car was "garaged" are in the background. The area was later to be used as the Co-op's coal yard and eventually for a new Co-op store. This area has now been converted into a small shopping precinct.

Shaw Methodists on Market Street in 1890.

From the Middle Ages until the eighteenth century, church floors consisted of bare earth, covered with layers of rushes to provide protection from the damp. Seating was only provided from the fifteenth century onwards. From this the annual rush cart festival developed.

At first the rushes were carried in bundles, then brought on sledges which were piled high like a haystack, and finally they were brought on a cart with wheels. In 1789 five rush carts went to Shaw Chapel. As many as seven have been recorded. They came from all over the township; Whitfield, Low Crompton, High Crompton, Narrowgate Brow, Crompton Fold, Nook and Laneside. The carts toured the township before proceeding to the chapel. On arrival, a bell was rung and a payment made to the first to arrive.

In 1826, following an outbreak of power loom breaking earlier in the year, William Rowbottom recorded in his diary: "There was a cart from Shaw in wich was placed a pair of looms, on wich a person was weaving."

These two photographs were taken in 1907 at High Crompton. This event may have been an attempt to revive the custom, as a history of Crompton written in 1902 reported that the custom of rush bearing had died out twenty or thirty years previously. In 1990 the rush cart festival was again revived and is now an annual event.

Shaw Wakes, 1906. The Market Place with Moorfield Mill in the background.

The Wakes holidays traditionally started on the first Saturday after the 13th August also known as Old Lammas Day. The name Lammas was derived from the old Saxon word Llaf Day meaning loaf day. The custom was to offer loaves, made from locally grown wheat, at the church on the day it was cleared of its old rushes and new ones laid down. In 1961 the Wakes holidays were changed to commence on the Saturday before the last Saturday in June. The Wakes were well known for Fairs with travelling shows and stalls.

SHAW WAKE
Tune, "Hokey Pokey"

Cum lay aside yur wheel un loom,
   Yur ploo un sythe un hay rake
Don on yur Sunday clooas un shoon,
   Then hey my lads for Shay Wake!

Shay Wake! Shay Wake!
   Then hey my lads for Shay Wake!
Shay Wake! Shay Wake!
   Then hey my lads for Shay Wake!

Thur's flying boxus, boats, and shows,
   Un fruit, un pies, un tay cakes,
Un rush carts covert o'er wi' gowd,
   Thur's every thin ut Shay Wake.
          Shay Wake, &c.

Look, here's a wolf un lion grim,
   A monkey un a say snake,
Wild pigs un bulls un ellefants,
   Un crokodiles ut Shay Wake.
          Shay Wake, &c.

Here's a pig cun wissle tunes,
   Un maggots like a jay spake,
Red herrins con yur fortin tell,
   But this is nowt ut Shay Wake.
          Shay Wake, &c.

Th' wenches kewert ith flyin box,
   Aloft ith air thur way take,
Un grin un laugh, it feels so queer,
   Furt fly so hee ut Shay Wake.
          Shay Wake, &c.

Crompton Cycle and Horse parade, 25th July 1903. This fancy dress parade was held in aid of Crompton Sick Nursing Association and the local Ambulance Corps. The main streets, through which the competitors paraded, were decorated with flags and bunting.

There were over 20 competitions to enter, ranging from lady cyclists in character, comic characters, Boy's Brigades, tableaux on cycles [left], gentlemen in character and juvenile characters which included Boy Blue, Bo-Peep, and Robin Hood. Music was provided by Shaw Brass Band, Royton Brass Band and Crompton Concertina Band.

The parade [above] gathered together behind the cricket club. On the left is the horse ambulance and to the right the nurses' entry with two nurses attending to a "sick" person.

Left: Two of the entries for the various competitions.

The horse ambulance [above] in 1903, with driver Albert Wild at Crompton Cricket Club. The first horse ambulance was presented to Crompton Council on 11th November 1899 by Superintendent McQueen of the County Police. The money for its purchase was raised by public subscription collected by the police and a grant from the Police Sports Fund. The ambulance was built by Messrs Wilson and Stockall of Bury. One of its innovative features was the body structure, which hung low on a cranked mail patent axle, to allow for easy access to the vehicle. During the First World War, Crompton Council found it difficult to get the ambulance maintained. In 1917 a motor ambulance with a Studebaker chassis and body built by Wilson and Stockall was purchased jointly by Crompton and Royton Urban District Councils for use within the two authorities.

The new ambulance [left] outside Crompton Town Hall.

The Boer War Peace Celebrations [left] on the Market ground. Moorfield Mill is to the left and the Swimming Baths to the right. There was great rejoicing in Shaw on Sunday 1st June 1902 after news had reached the town of the end of the hostilities in South Africa. The following evening, Shaw Brass Band paraded through the town which was decked with flags. Three thousand people assembled on the Market Ground to attend a meeting called by the chairman of the Council in honour of the peace declaration.

Coronation activities were curtailed in 1902, when the ceremony was cancelled owing to the illness of Edward VII. Arrangements which could be postponed were, but the scholars' tea, old folks' dinner and the lighting of the bonfire [left] at Doghill all took place on 26th June.

Celebrations recommenced on 9th August with an ox and pig roast [below] in the market ground. The chef, Mr George Luckett of Stratford-on-Avon, was well-known for roasting whole oxen and pigs which were placed on spits and turned slowly. The roasting commenced at 6am and the meat was ready by 11.30am. A marquee had been erected and was used to serve the public with portions of the meat. Demand was such that all the portions had been eaten by 3.30pm!

The following day, there was a procession by most of the Sunday School scholars through the town to the Market Ground where a service was held. Altogether 3,000 children took part and 2,000 adults witnessed the proceedings.

As part of an official two day visit to the Oldham area, Her Majesty Queen Elizabeth II and HRH the Duke of Edinburgh visited Lilac Mill on 22nd October 1954. They were received by the Lord Lieutenant of the County Palatine of Lancashire, the Right Honourable the Earl of Derby MC. The Queen was escorted around the mill by the Managing Director, Fred Wood. She is seen here watching cops coming off the conditioning machine after being dipped. In the evening there was a bonfire on Salts Street playground and a firework display to commemorate her visit.

The custom of "Beating the Bounds" began in medieval times as a means of defining the boundaries of the township to a population, the majority of whom could neither read nor write. Members of the local populace would gather and be led by those who were familiar with the boundaries.

The custom was revived in the late nineteenth century and has taken place, with several interruptions due to the wars, at least once every seven years ever since.

Two of the more unusual aspects of beating Crompton's bounds were to swim across Besom Hill reservoir and climb over the roof of the King's Arms pub at Grains Bar, thus following the exact boundary line. Now however the reservoir has been lowered and a back door constructed at the pub, so alleviating the need to carry out these unique aspects of the event. The bounds were last beaten in September 1993.

Kate's body was found in front of the double doors to the left.
The building was opposite the old Greenfield Mill.

Kate Garrity, aged 17, of Mosshey, was found strangled to death on 20th December 1905. She had gone out the previous evening at 8.10pm to fetch beer from the Blue Bell for her father, who found her body hidden amongst sacks against a factory wall the following morning.

Jack Griffiths, a former boyfriend, was arrested and formally charged with her murder. His trial at Manchester Assizes, took place in February 1906. He was found guilty and hanged. Kate was buried in Moston cemetery.

Crompton Urban District Council constructed two sewage disposal works; one at Newhey in 1889 and the other in 1896 at Low Crompton [above]. The latter was enlarged between 1921 and 1923. Low Crompton works closed in 1973 when the system was connected to the newly constructed Thorp relief sewer in Royton.